Spines, Horns, and Armor:

ANIMAL WEAPONS AND DEFENSES

BY JODY SULLIVAN RAKE

CONTENT CONSULTANT:
JACKIE GAI, DVM
ZOO AND EXOTIC ANIMAL VETERINARIAN

READING CONSULTANT:
BARBARA J. FOX
READING SPECIALIST
PROFESSOR EMERITUS
NORTH CAROLINA STATE UNIVERSITY

CAPSTONE PRESS
a capstone imprint

Blazers is published by Capstone Press,
1710 Roe Crest Drive, North Mankato, Minnesota 56003.
www.capstonepub.com

Books published by Capstone Press are manufactured with paper
containing at least 10 percent post-consumer waste.

Library of Congress Cataloging-in-Publication Data
Rake, Jody Sullivan.
    Spines, horns, and armor : animal weapons and defenses / by Jody Sullivan Rake.
    p. cm. — (Blazers. animal weapons and defenses.)
    Includes bibliographical references and index.
    Summary: "Describes how animals use spines, horns, and armor as weapons and defenses"
—Provided by publisher.
    ISBN 978-1-4296-6505-6 (library binding)
    ISBN 978-1-4296-8011-0 (paperback)
    1. Spines (Zoology)—Juvenile literature. 2. Horns—Juvenile literature. 3. Armored animals—
Juvenile literature. I. Title.
QL385.R35 2012
591.47—dc23   2011034686

Editorial Credits
Mandy Robbins, editor; Kyle Grenz, designer; Svetlana Zhurkin, media researcher;
    Laura Manthe, production specialist

Photo Credits
Alamy: Ariadne Van Zandbergen, 18–19; Dreamstime: Alan Jeffery, 24–25, Briankieft, 8–9,
Jacob Melrose, 28–29, Mikephotos, 22–23, Nicholashan, 20–21, Nikita Rogul, 26–27;
iStockphoto: Kipp Schoen, 16–17; SeaPics: Doug Perrine, cover (top); Shutterstock:
Johan Swanepoel, 4–5, Johan Swanepoel, 14–15, NatalieJean, 10–11, NH, cover (bottom),
Steve Lovegrove, 12–13, tratong, 6–7

Printed in the United States of America in
Stevens Point, Wisconsin.
102011   006404WZS12

TABLE OF CONTENTS

STAY AWAY!

Surviving in the wild is a battle, and many animals come armed. Sharp spines, piercing horns, and tough armor protect some animals from **predators**.

predator—an animal that hunts other animals for food

LIVING PIN CUSHIONS

A porcupine's spines are called quills. One porcupine has thousands of quills. These spiky weapons cause painful wounds.

☆ FIERCE FACT ☆

Quills are made of keratin. This is the same substance that makes up hair and fingernails.

Puffer fish are covered in pointed spines. When they feel threatened, these fish blow up like balloons. Then their spines look even bigger. Predators don't want to eat a huge ball of spines!

10

Be careful not to step on a sea urchin. These prickly creatures have sharp spines. Some have spines that are thin like needles. Others have thick spines like pointy pencils.

Some sea urchins have venom in their spines. This poisonous liquid is released into their victims.

Most lizards are scaly and rough. But the thorny devil is prickly. Some of its spines are even covered with smaller spikes!

The color of the thorny devil can change to match the color of the soil it is walking on.

THE POWER OF HORNS

Black rhinos have strong, pointed horns on their snouts. Like the porcupine's quills, a rhino's horns are made of keratin. The black rhino's front horn grows to about 3 feet (1 meter) long.

The world record for the longest black rhino horn is 5 feet (1.5 meters) long.

Male bighorn sheep have two heavy curved horns on their heads. The sheep use their horns for **ramming**. Male bighorns have fierce head-butting battles during **mating season**. The winner gets to mate with a female.

ram—to crash into something with great force

mating season—a time of year when animals seek out a male or female partner

The scimitar-horned oryx is a type of antelope. Each of its long, curved horns looks like a sword called a scimitar. The horns usually reach 3 to 4 feet (1 to 1.2 meters).

The male rhinoceros beetle uses its horns to battle other males for a **mate**. It can also use its horns to dig itself into a hole to hide from attackers.

mate—the male or female partner in a pair of animals

ARMED FOR BATTLE

Hard bony plates cover an armadillo's body. These strong keratin plates protect armadillos from predators.

★ FIERCE FACT ★

Armadillo is Spanish for "little armored one."

All rhinos are thick-skinned. But
the skin of the Indian rhino offers the
most protection. Its tough **hide** hangs
like a suit of armor. This thick, bumpy
skin protects the rhino from predators
and other rhinos' horns.

hide—the skin of an animal

Only land turtles can pull their heads and legs into their shells. Sea turtles cannot do this.

Like all reptiles, turtles have scaly skin. They also have tough shells. Turtles curl up inside their shells. There they are protected from the snapping jaws and sharp claws of attackers.

A crab's shell is like plate armor on the outside of its body. It is called an **exoskeleton**. Defenses like this help crabs and many other animals survive another day.

exoskeleton—a hard covering on the outside of an animal

GLOSSARY

exoskeleton (ek-soh-SKE-luh-tuhn)—the hard covering on the outside of an animal

hide (HIDE)—the skin of an animal

mate (MATE)—the male or female partner in a pair of animals

mating season (MAYT-ing SEE-zuhn)—the time of year when animals seek out a male or female partner

predator (PRED-uh-tur)—an animal that hunts other animals for food

ram (RAM)—to crash into something with great force

★ READ MORE ★

Mitchell, Susan K. *Animals with Awesome Armor: Shells, Scales, and Exoskeletons.* Amazing Animal Defenses. Berkeley Heights, N.J.: Enslow, 2009.

Pryor, Kimberley Jane. *Amazing Armor.* Animal Attack and Defense. New York: Marshall Cavendish Benchmark, 2010.

Stone, Lynn M. *Snouts, Spines, and Scutes.* What Animals Wear. Vero Beach, Fla.: Rourke Pub., 2009.

INTERNET SITES

FactHound offers a safe, fun way to find Internet sites related to this book. All of the sites on FactHound have been researched by our staff.

Here's all you do:

Visit *www.facthound.com*

Type in this code: 9781429665056

www.FactHound.com

Super-cool stuff!

Check out projects, games and lots more at
www.capstonekids.com

INDEX